GEO SPIRIT

For Environment & Earth Leadership

SAI BHASKAR N. REDDY

GEO SPIRIT

For Environment & Earth Leadership

1st Edition, 2016

This is an 'Open Knowledge' book as declared by the author.
Dr. Sai Bhaskar N. Reddy, 2016
saibhaskarnakka@gmail.com

Note: The author drew sketches and mostly took the photos presented in this book.

For 'The Earth'

CONTENTS

INTRODUCTION

Geo Spirit is about everything that one strives for the harmony and well-being of one's inner space and the outer space on this Earth.

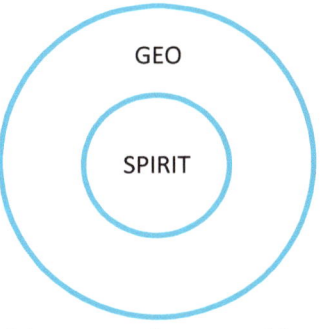

Geo Spirit is the consciousness on earth. "Geo Spirit" consists of two realms - "Geo" is the Earth, including biotic and abiotic worlds and "Spirit" is the consciousness of peace, freedom and harmony for oneself and everything else on this earth. Geo Spirit is the ever pervading consciousness on the earth at all levels, including the sub-atomic level.

The human beings are the single species disharmonizing the earth. Geo Spirit is for understanding and getting connected to the earth. Geo Spirit ultimately aims at the oneness of the earth integrating and harmonizing the diversities. Consistent earth leadership is needed, to understand and participate in these processes for positive change. One should be sensitive and should be the means and cause of earth resources sustainability.

Spirit manifests in oneness and freedom. Earth is a single living thing; in which we are also a part. Geo Spirit helps to understand why the earth has provided us everything to celebrate another day. One should also strive and question, why I am born on this earth? If I am living, what is the difference I can make? If there is no positive change that one is causing, then there is not much meaning to one's life. That is the spirit of living.

Through Geo Spirit, one's awareness, sensitivity, knowledge, understanding, actions, and spirit become relevant to the harmony and well-being on earth and the infinite space. Through the "GEO SPIRIT," one could realize the possibility of becoming an "EARTH LEADER.". Each individual is an earth leader, when one is able to unleash their potential to bring the positive change on this earth. Ultimately, whatever one does, it is important to get connected to the earth.

THE EARTH

When the universe came into existence, the earth became one of the living planets with life. Life is matter and energy with consciousness.

The earth is the single 'living thing'. One should understand the intricate relationships between various biotic and abiotic worlds which made this earth. Earth is our only space upon which we all live. Earth is the space bargained to live from future life on the earth.

The earth leader should be conscious of every action and its impact. In true love there is no reason, one should love the truth and strive for strive for any change that is sustainable.

One of the intelligent and critical species evolved on earth are Human beings. This species alone in the last 150 years has been responsible for all the destruction that is happening on the earth.

If one thinks I belong to a nation or a region they are mean and smaller, but if one thinks I belong to "The Earth,"-by accepting the whole - they are bigger in life. Wherever one is there in time and space, they own that place. People living on earth discriminate and own only parts of the earth. Why can't we love and own the earth as a whole, rather representing it in parts? The real spirit of an earth leader is to love each and every part of the earth. If everyone loves the earth, which is the only space to live, there would be peace and development of one and all. The spirit of the earth is the spirit of you. You take care of the earth; the earth will take care of you.

Ironically people strive to own properties like land. They declare that this piece of land belongs to me. Is it true? From whom do they separate the piece of earth and for how long do they own it? Can every living thing (including insects and microbes) on this earth, claim that this land belongs to them? Land and resources were there even before the human beings evolved on this earth. And the earth would last even beyond human extinction. To be precise, we are mere guests on this earth.

How can one own the earth in parts through the paper currency notes? How can one get collateral loans by pledging pieces of this earth? Then whose land it is? It is 'our land' and not 'my land'.

Some people have become too mean, they say unless you love this piece of land - country or a region - you cannot live here? The piece of land is so small when compared to the whole earth. Loving the Earth is more important than loving in pieces. If 'The Gods' pervade beyond the geographical boundaries and love the whole universe, why people are mean to love just pieces of land.

GOAL

The goal is the ultimate means to achieve greater change. Peace, Love, Happiness, and Freedom are the fundamental building blocks which comprise goals. Spirit is the basic innate energy which should always be active in one's life to achieve the goal. Spirit is a precursor to goal.

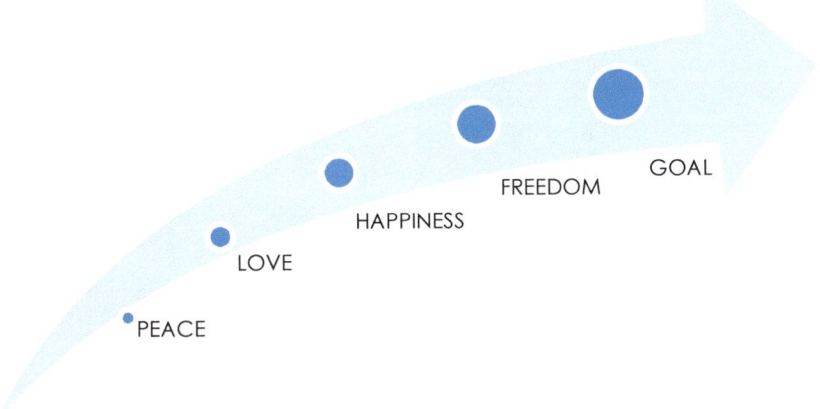

Intention and initiative arenecessary to realize one's goal. Maximum performance is needed to achieve challenging goals. Working for oneself is not the goal.

If young people set their goals at an early age, they would have more time and capacity to change the world. The beauty of life is the goal that guides and drives every action of a person. Young children consider that their teachers are knowledgeable and wise, so they respect them. Many children say that they want to be a 'Teacher' when they grow up. If teachers are asked - What is their Goal in life? Many of them don't have a straight answer. If teachers don't have a life goal, how can they inspire the children towards a goal? Teachers bereft of a goal would never be able to teach a child what a 'Goal' is?

Understanding the purpose of life at an early age makes life more valuable. Children being young may not comprehend 'goal for the life,' they can have short-rungoals. Goals can change over time and space for children, but after reaching a certain age, say between the age group 12 years and 18 years, they should understand and decide a goal and endeavorto achieve it.

The goal is like trying to reach the top of a peak. The time spent in reaching the peak is more than time spent at the peak. Achieving the goal implies all the processes are followed. An ant is never seen sleeping under a tree in spite of securing its food. An ant's goal in life is to the well-being and prosperity of the community. A goal is ultimate and there is no loss in striving, one achieves it or will end up somewhere on the way.

The profession chosen need not be the goal, but the purpose and values around the result describe the Goal.

FREEDOM

Great leaders always loved freedom, lived with freedom and strived for the freedom of everyone. Some of the great leaders who stood by example are Henry Thoreau, M. K. Gandhi, and Martin Luther King.

Freedom is innate. Freedom to choose and do what one loves is real-life. The way one prefers to dress before sleep is one of the simplest expressions of the freedom. The so-called civilized developed and urban people have less freedom than an indigenous tribe living in areas close to nature.

Those who want freedom, they already have, need not declare that I want freedom. People can fight for independence and rights, but not for freedom, unless they are slaves or convicts. Freedom is always there with oneself. Others can't give someone's freedom. If someone wants to walk without shoes, it is their own freedom. They don't need approval from someone. Freedom is always there for everyone and everywhere. The chance to choose one's destiny is freedom; it never comes without a price. With freedom also comes duty and responsibility. Other than the humans, all life on earth has more freedom.

In today's world, every person is born with some debt, distributed per capita by their country. The debt of almost all the nations is increasing every year because today's development model (both for nations or individuals) is based on credit.

People started enjoying things of future. We are enjoying the "present-future" costing our generations to come. Present-future, means, present day one is enjoying resources meant for future generations. For example, say about 40 years back one would have owned a house at about 50 years' age, that too with life-long savings. In the recent times, through access to loans by young people of age 25 to 30 years owna house.

This leads to over-exploitation of resources at present at the cost of future generations. Such things are possible only by human beings. All other living things live in the present, but man is able to exploit the future. This system leads to imbalance on earth. This is only a "Hype", already we are witness to countries' economies collapsing. Collateral credit on earth resources is one such means. If younger generations are paying the bills of older generations, then where is the chance to be born with freedom?

EARTH LEADER

Everyone is an 'Earth Leader' – all those committed to the earth's sustainability.One who possess Sensitivity, Humility, Truthfulness, Empathy and Commitment is a leader.

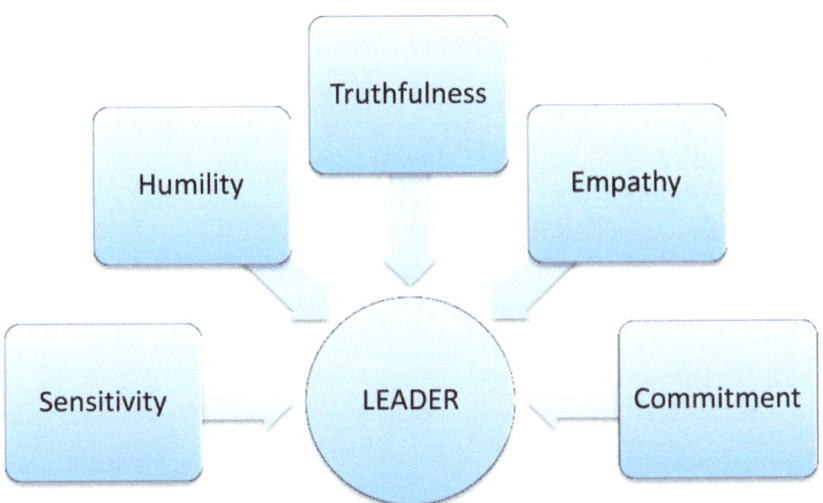

Education should nurture humility and simplicity in a person, rather makeone complex and exclusive. Today's school's system provides knowledge and some skills but does not provide understanding and space for leadership. Knowledge alone need not guide one's actions towards the well-being of all and harmony.

A real leader sensitizes and makes everyone equally responsible. The problem becomes our problem rather than my problem or your problem. Leaders have their own personal issues, still they take up common and bigger problems.

One cannot live for oneself. 'One for All - All for One'- every earth leader should understand this. One cannot live without the support of the environment and also one cannot live for oneself. One can only live for others and everything on this earth. Everyone and everythingare part of the whole. Everyone living on the earth can work only for the earth.

The 'sustainability' of societies and civilizations are defined in the space of leadership. There are many leaders and each leader is for a cause. The greater the cause, which is for the commongood, it is more important for an earth leader to lead. A small farmer in a village who adopted eco-friendly practices and produced more crop yield, in spite of the limited capitals (such as human, social, economic, natural, physical and environmental) is also an earth leader.

True leaders have the freedom and strive for the freedom of one and all. A leader's personal goal is always within the common goal. A great leader sets the high goals, which are not so easy to achieve in one's lifetime. A great leader inspires everyone around and becomes a source for the emergence of great leaders. A leader is not the one who considers the people as sheep to follow him or her blindly. There is no master and slave relationship in real leadership. Followers believe the values that the leader is representing and if necessary do challenge the same leader when fails to espouse that cause. Earth leadership provides the space for everyone to be a leader and not just one or few.

The common goals to be achieved is not someone's job. Therefore, a leader inspires and in the space of "everyone a great leader", strives for the achievement of common goals.

A leader comes forward to take a risk. A great leader should also be knowledgeable, innovative, and skilled. To be competent, the leader should continuously learn and have domain knowledge in the areas of one's work. Only with knowledge and right skills, they are able to provide direction to others, lead the team and the followers.

A leader's ecological footprint should be small. They should lead an environmentally conscious life, and be the role models for others to follow. Leaders living in extravagant buildings while in power should remember that there are many homeless people. The life cycle of the excess spaces used by an individual has an enormous impact on the environment and ecology.

A great leader is an artist, envisions on the canvas of time and creates a beautiful future. Great leaders have a great vision.

A leader always believes that "A Leader is not a Leader." The leader is the one who empowers everyone including the followers. A leader inspires and sees the people around them as great leaders. A leader never creates emptiness when he leaves. In 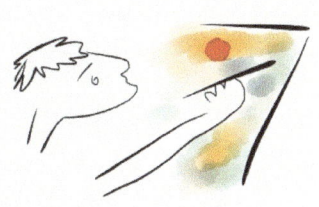 the absence of a great leader, there should not be chaos. A leader does not suck the power of people around them to become a powerful leader.

Many leaders appear to have become leaders, by creating followers. Through the followers and supporters, some might attain the position of a leader. There could be some great potential leaders among followers too. A great leaders work and spirit inspire the future generations.

Achieving the common goal by all means is more important for a leader, than reaching one's personal goals.

Leaders have several strengths. Often leaders are great orators, their power of speech and lucid expressions are also important to achieve results. The character, experience and credibility of a leader are also important to cause great results. While striving to achieve the common goals, one should be down-to-earth.

Leaders are also means of innovation, inspiration and change in any walk of life they are -in every school, college, agency, institute, system, project, and program. The role and responsibility of a leader are mainly explicit in the times of crisis. Everyone is a great leader – the size of the challenge and impact caused are also important measures to understand their contribution.

Characteristics of an earth leader
- The common goal is bigger and more important than the self-goal.
- Takes up challenges in all situations.
- Prepares in advance foreseeing the future.
- Gives scope for younger leadership, when they are shaped for the task.
- Gives up positions, if needed.
- Aspires for higher leadership.
- Does not do politics for positions.
- Is the last one to leave in case of a vulnerable situation.
- Responsible and takes all kinds of risks.

GEO SPIRIT PRINCIPLES

One should be conscious of the three aspects of life, i.e., Spirit, Knowledge, and Action.

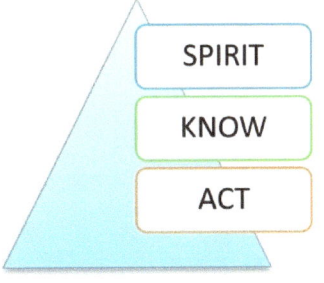

Action or Karma is the most fundamental thing to perform in life. The action is decisive and essential to cause results. Action manifests mostly in the material world as it is mainly tangible. To act is most fundamental for any life on earth. With practice and skills, one can perform and cause greater results. Action should be positive and cause least negative impacts on the earth. The purpose of acquiring knowledge is also important. Above all understanding is important in life. Our education system must impart knowledge, beyond actual use. To change the world, knowledge and understanding are useful and one can have knowledge of many things. Being human, having wisdom and Knowledge are the basis for understanding. Spirit is above all, i.e., action and knowledge. Spirit guides to achieve right knowledge and act wisely to cause greater results. An earth leader's spirit changes the world.

The earth leaders for change could focus on various components of Geo Spirit such as Energy, Water, Habitat, Nature, Health, Education, etc. These are some of the most relevant and fundamental concerns and issuesaffecting life on earth. Earth leaders could be from all walks of life, and they could choose any area related to their individual spirit, knowledge and skills.

An earth leader should practice and preach. Leading by example is the prerequisite. There are different models to begin with. The earth leaders should declare at least one tree as mother tree and strive to protect. This is apart from conserving and planting trees. Geo Spirit Centre gives space for an earth leader to understand and learn. Geo Spirit communes are the spaces for living with other earth leaders. They are also centers of learning from the earth leaders and get inspired by their work. Geo Spirit Groves need to be declared independently or they should be part of every Geo Spirit Center or Geo Spirit Commune. These centers would inspire many earth leaders to strive for a global commune living with least ecological footprint. Everyone with Geo Spirit would ultimately create a peaceful global commune.

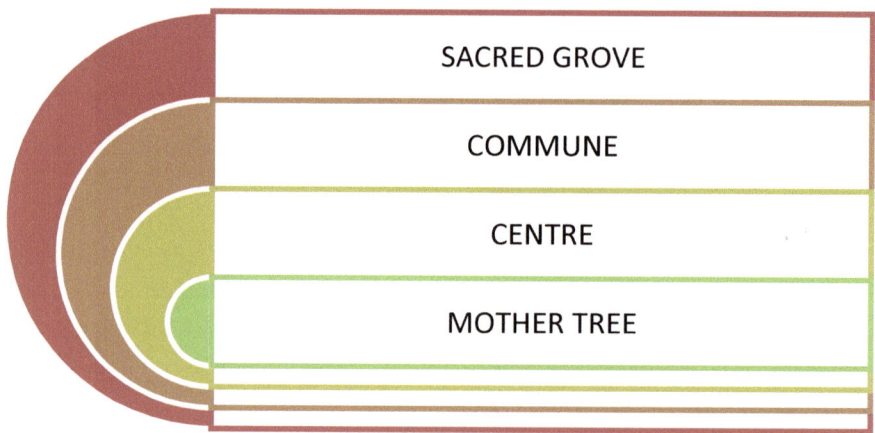

GEO SPIRIT MOTHER TREE

Mother tree is any plant species young or old, that a community promises to let it have a complete life with freedom. Existing trees could be identified and declared by the community as mother trees. Individuals or organizations could register the piece of land where the tree exists and declare the tree as mother tree.

Declaring old trees as mother trees has greater value. The old trees living in an area establish connections with all other trees through roots and fungi. They also become a host for a wide variety of local fauna. Around them, several other plant species live in symbiotic relationship and harmony. The people living around also establish an emotional relationship as they cherish memories of living and growing with it. They are the mute witness to all the happenings in the environment and the changes happening over years.

Bodhi tree under which Gautama Buddha, is said to have achieved enlightenment is still existing. Its saplings are propagated throughout the world with great reverence.

GEO SPIRIT CENTRE

The Geo Spirit Centre is a declared place with least human interventions, giving space for nature to flourish. An area with a concentration of highest biodiversity of local species, an abode for plants, animals, and microbes. These places become learning centers on issues relevant to earth. Each center could focus on specific topicsrelevant to the immediate geography and other relatedissues. Demonstration and exhibition of good practices and technologies motivate the earth leaders to adopt and practice. They also become the learning centers for visiting people. To establish a Geo Spirit Centre, the area required could be as little as half-acreor more. Only a few individuals could stay there during capacity building, but are not meant for a permanent stay.

Geo Spirit centers could be declared by everyone and everywhere. Geo Spirit centres could be farmer's fields; private lands; educational institutions; religious places and other common areas.

Benefits to the immediate environment because of Geo Spirit Centers are:

- [ ] Space hosts a variety of birds, reptiles, mammals and other fauna.
- [ ] Heaven for the soil microbes a must requirement for keeping the soils alive, rather dead.
- [ ] The biodiversity of plants is the host for fauna and also an excellent resource of the genetic pool.

☐ The neighboring fields require fewer inputs for their crop management because of the above aspects.

These centers are a declaration by the people who own those spaces for the earth - i.e., Geo Spirit.

Geo Spirit Centers declared by the author is at Peddamaduru Village, Devaruppala Mandal, Warangal District, Telangana, India. In a 0.5-acre land, this place has 200 species of flora. A biomass stoves museum and a biochar production facility are existing. Green building concepts are used in the construction of the buildings. An office is constructed with soil (adobe), biochar bricks are used in the construction of the museum cum training hall, stoves production workshop and a kitchen lab (for testing stoves also used for cooking food). It has the facility to train 50 people. About 10 people could stay overnight comfortably.

GEO SPIRIT COMMUNE

A commune is a large gathering of people sharing a common life; sharing common interests, and resources. The Geo Spirit communes would have like-minded people working forthe earth – They are the earth leaders. There could be many Geo Spirit communes in every part of the earth.

Geo Spirit communes are the places around Geo Spirit centers for people to live in harmony with nature. The living would be minimalistic based on the spirit of earth, with least impact on resources. The written constitution or set of rules are derived based on the principles. The constitution is the basis of the commune of earth leaders living in Geo Spirit.

A commune - the French word appearing in the 12th century from Medieval Latin *communia*, means a large gathering of people sharing a common life. From Latin *communis*, that is things held in common is an intentional community of people living together, sharing common interests, property, possessions, resources, and, in some communes, work, and income.

The notion of a utopia—a perfect, egalitarian, and harmonious paradise on earth—has been a recurring theme in literature and storytelling for hundreds of years. It all started with the philosopher Plato's book Republic, and it's since been expressed in other books including Thomas More's Utopia and Edward Bellamy's Looking

Backward, as well as in films like Lost Horizon and Things to Come. This discussion of an ideal and peaceful society has encouraged many people to try and bring these ideas into reality through spiritual communes and new forms of community organization.[1]

A Geo Spirit Commune is a permanent sort of place for people to set a role model by living with principles, they are:

Preamble

- ☐ The earth is one living thing.
- ☐ One for all, all for one.
- ☐ One cannot own the earth; we are only trustees.
- ☐ Living in harmony with nature.
- ☐ The ecological footprint should be small, by adopting the minimalistic approach.

---

[1] http://www.toptenz.net/top-10-experimental-towns-and-communes.php

- Respecting environment, ecology, and biodiversity.
- Striving for earth leadership for a sustainable future.

Space

- The Geo Spirit Commune (GSC) is declared by the members who own the space.
- The Geo Spirit Centre or The Earth Centre is an essential part of the Geo Spirit Commune.
- The Members of the Geo Spirit Commune are the "Earth Leaders."
- The commune has the Earth leader's habitats.
- The Geo Spirit Commune has a common boundary
- The Geo Spirit Commune has a common water source/s for the whole commune.
- Roads within The Geo Spirit Commune would be laid as and when only required.
- Internal mobility is by walk or bicycles.
- Planting trees - a minimum of one plant per square meter.
- Conservation of native plants.
- To plant and to cut trees the approval of commune members is required.
- A place with a concentration of highest biodiversity of local species, an abode for plants, animals, microbes and also an excellent resource of the genetic pool.
- Collective protection and management of plants.
- Cultivation of medicinal plants, vegetables, fruits, etc.
- Independent solar power sources for lighting and other domestic requirements.
- Regular power from grid only for non-negotiable requirements.
- No more than 25% of the land owned by members should be use for construction.
- Construction of eco-friendly habitations and architectural designs to be approved by commune members.
- Shared kitchen and healthy local food.
- Sharedlibrary
- Eco-friendly technologies and practices - good stoves, biogas,

compost, biochar, non-pesticide management, organic, permaculture, water harvesting, waste management, etc.

- To transfer or to sell any piece of land in the commune, approval of the commune members is required.
- The constitution rules apply to all the members and their heirs, affiliate members, visitors, and guests.
- The Commune would be registered as a society.

Membership

- Qualifications to be a member of the centre - Must have contributed to theenvironment, development, social service, education, public service and relevant areas.
- Core members own a piece of land in thecentre and Affiliate Members are those affiliated to the centre.
- All members of the centre are the Earth Leaders.
- All the commondecisions are taken based on the approval by at least 50% of the commune members.

GEO SPIRIT GROVES

Sacred groves are existing all over the globe. They are similar to the proposed Geo Spirit Groves, where people conserve nature with values and spirituality. In parts of India, there is a temple mostly found in every sacred grove. They are also referred to by different names in various regions of India. Sacred groves occur in a variety  of places – from scrub forests in the Thar Desert of Rajasthan maintained by the *Bishnois*, to rainforests in the Western Ghats of Kerala. Himachal Pradesh in the north and Kerala in the south are specifically known for their scores of sacred groves. The *Kodavas* of Karnataka alone maintained over 1000 sacred groves in their region. The Gujjar people of Rajasthan have a unique practice of neem (Azadirachta indica) planting and worshipping as the abode of God Devnarayan. Thus, a Gujjar settlement appears like a human-inhabited sacred grove. Similarly, Mangar Bani the last surviving natural forest of Delhi is protected by Gujjar's of the nearby area. Around 14,000 sacred groves have been reported from all over India, which acts as reservoirs of rare fauna, and more often are a habitat for rare flora, amid rural and even urban settings. Experts believe that the total number of sacred groves could be as high as 100,000.

Some of the more famous groves are the *Kavus* of Kerala, which are located in the Western Ghats and has enormous biodiversity; and the Law of Meghalaya – sacred groves associated with every village (two large groves being in Mawphlang and Mausmai) to appease the forest spirit.

Among the largest sacred groves of India are the ones in Hariyali, near Gauchar in Chamoli District of Uttarakhand, and the Deodar Grove in Shipin near Shimla in Himachal Pradesh. Kodagu, a small region of about 4000 km² in Karnataka, has over 1000 sacred groves.

One of the most important traditional functions of sacred groves was that it acted as a repository for various Ayurvedic medicines. Other uses involved a source of replenishable resources like fruits and honey. However, in most sacred groves it was taboo to hunt or chop wood. The vegetation cover helps reduce soil erosion and prevents desertification. The groves are often associated with ponds and streams and meet water requirements of local communities. They sometimes help in recharging aquifers as well.

In modern times, sacred groves have become biodiversity hotspots, as various species seek refuge in the areas due to progressive habitat destruction, and hunting. Sacred groves often contain plant and animal species that have become extinct in neighboring areas. They, therefore, harbor high genetic diversity. Besides this, sacred groves in urban landscapes act as "lungs" to the city as well, providing much-needed vegetation cover.

Threats to the grove include urbanization, over-exploitation of resources (like overgrazing and excessive fuelwood collection), and environmental destruction due to religious practices. Sometimes too many visitors to the sacred groves also disturb the sacred groves flora and fauna. While many of the groves are looked upon as abode of Hindu gods, in the recent past someof them have been partially cleared for construction of shrines and temples. Other threats to the sacred groves include invasions by invasive weeds like *Chromolaena odorata, Lantana camara,* and *Prosopis juliflora.*

Promoting Geo Spirit Groves has the highest value. It is a selfless declaration to conserve the nature. Everyone possessing land should allocate at least 10% of their land for the Geo Spirit Groves. Geo Spirit Groves should be a must even in the Geo Spirit Centers and Geo Spirit Communes. The individual farmers, corporate farmers, collectives, public gardens, parks, mining areas, etc., should also declare 10% of the land for the Geo Spirit Groves. It would be great if least intervention by human beings is there in the Geo Spirit Groves. Ideally, they should be the abode for all flora & fauna.

Before planting a tree, it is important to identify a tree for conservation and save a tree through protection.

GEO SPIRIT MEET

During Geo Spirit meets, the earth conscious people come together to experience earth, discuss, learn, and declare their goals and action plans. The declaration made by respective participants at the end of each Geo Spirit Meet is a self-declaration and voluntary. One's declaration is the most powerful thing. The facilitator only encourages and inspires for taking up the bigger challenge. The individual declarations are not recorded, nor meant to be monitored for the progress or results. The achievements and the results speak for themselves.

Declaring "GEO Spirit centers" and "Mother Trees" is one of the means to conserve biodiversity and most importantly the soil microbes.

The Geo Spirit meets can be organized everywhere, which inspires and motivates one to work for the determined cause. Such as, in the lush green forest areas, in the mountains, in a desert, at water bodies, in the slum areas, in the middle of the city, etc. Every part and place should inspire us as we love each and every part of the earth.

As avenue to conduct the Geo Spirit meet, any place on the earth could be selected. Preferably a place where there is less disturbance. For those interested in the environment and ecological challenges a natural area is preferred. Someone among the participants should declare a date and venue for the Geo Spirit Meet. The number of participants ideally could be around 30 people. To participate in a meet, the group size could be 5 to 50 people. The participants in the meets could be men, women, youth and children (above 12 years' age). It would be convenient to conduct meets for people with similar interests and age groups together, then a diverse and broad spectrum of individuals.

For all those willing to participate in the Geo Spirit meet, the commencement begins from the moment one has confirmed to join. Geo spirit is a continuous process and for lifelong.

Geo Spirit meets are not commercial. The participants should bear the cost of coming to the venue on their own. The local organization or coordinator declares the date and venue of Geo spirit meet. They take care of the food and local logistics. In the case of not being in a position to take care of logistics, the participants should share the cost. The Geo Spirit meets should be conducted with least expenditure and in a manner as simple as possible. The participation is more of commitment to the earth, rather an entertainment tour or adventure trip to the participants. All the participants should participate voluntarily and give a self-declaration for their life during participation.

Food and beverages served should preferably be same as closer to local traditions and customs. The stay would be mostly in the open and with least resources. A typical Geo Spirit meet, lasts about 24 hours.

Individuals should wear any comfortable dress with accessories such as jackets or sweaters or shawls or caps etc. to protect themselves from the weather. Should preferably wear shoes. Should have a small tent if possible. A blanket or a sleeping bag is optional based on the need. Should not bring books, music players, laptops, playing gadgets, etc. Before coming for the Geo Spirit meet should read some good books or watch videos relevant to their goals. A few experiences from the Geo Spirit meets conducted by the author are shared below.

NATURE

One of the memorable, Geo Spirit meets was organized in the Nallamalai forest, near Yerragondapalem, Prakasam District, Andhra Pradesh State, India.

Nallamalai forest is an important part of theEastern Ghats covering parts of Telangana and Andhra Pradesh States. It is hosting the largest tiger reserve in Asia. The rock formations comprise mainly of quartzite and shales. The biodiversity of tropical dry deciduous forests and fauna makes it most beautiful. The forest trees with various forms in the background of quartzite add to the beauty. The streams and nalascreating beautiful valleys, gravel bed streams with adjoining magnificent trees made this place a paradise.

It was in the first week of February 2012 one of the Geo Spirit meets was organized with the support of an NGO working with local tribal communities. The participants from Hyderabad arrived one day ahead at Yerragondapalem. It is a small town. There were 18 participants from Hyderabad and 12 Chenchu tribes. After having breakfast started on a tractor trailer. To avoid the heavy vibrations on the rough forest path, the trailer was half filled with sand.

On the way saw Veerabhadra Swamy Temple, an ancient temple at Ganjivaripalli (16.033085, 79.200097), from here onwards the road towards Palutla (about 30 km away) is a rough earth road with gravel and small stones. The road and stream channel run parallel. Palutla is known for cotton cultivation, along the way saw cotton sticking to the branches of the trees when the vehicles laden with cotton moved.

On the way, had lunch with types of Sorghum rotis, i.e., plain roti, salted roti and hot roti (salt and pickle added while preparation). This is the traditional food of the local Chenchu tribes.

By around 4:00 pm we reached a place called 'Peddamma Bayyanna temple' Camp (16.097315, 79.124722) which is about 20 km away from Ganjivaripalli on the way to Palutla where Tribal people worship. Only the basic facilities were available such as a hand pump for water, one solar light and a bamboo hut built by the forest department.

Four groups were formed with two to three tribal people in each group and were asked to transect walk in different directions. All the groups' members were instructed, not to go more than one km. All the teams have collected information on local biodiversity. After returning the teams shared their understanding and experience, against the sun setting over the hills.

In all the Geo Spirit meets modest food is preferred. On the way, we had crispy Rotis prepared with Sorghum flour, added with garlic, chilipaste, and salt. For dinner, the food was cooked on three stone stoves. A local variety brown rice and vegetable curries were prepared and served. For the first time tasted i.e. Deodar leaf curry, Istsapa kaya curry, and Medikaya curry – it was like egg scramble in appearance and taste. Next day breakfast was the tasty Ragi-ball and rice with sambar.

The Chenchu tribe living in the forest were more knowledgeable. It was decided to learn from them first about their life in the forest, wildlife encounters or sightings, and any other stories. Tried to know their aspirations. Many of them do not have any intuition to amasswealth but preferred to survive through what mother earth provides.

They are afraid of tigers which were rare to find. Leopards were most ferocious, but above all the bears caused more injuries and killed people living in the forest.

After breakfast, the team went to banks of a stream for appreciation and experiencing nature. Each one participated in the Geo Spirit exercises gets connected with nature throughthe activities such as –being Calm; bathing in the gentle rays of morning Sun;walking barefoot with closed eyes and experiencing the mother earth; hearing sounds of nature;listening to the calls of jungle fowls and birds; appreciating the trees; hugging trees, feeling the texture of tree parts; observing insects and birds; smelling surroundings; etc.

Having born on this earth experiencing the environment and being part of the earth enriches one's spirit.

In the morning, the tribals prepared breakfast. By the time we all were hungry. We thought they would serve the breakfast immediately after cooking. But we were asked to wait for half an hour. They said that they would serve us only after offering prasadam (the sweet dish of rice and coconuts) to their gods. One of them had taken a bath, took the food in fresh leaves and placed before the stones (idols) as an offering. These stones locally available in millions were simple slabs. Although they have no significant shape, theypasted dots of red vermillion over yellow turmeric colored on them. They had specific names for each stone. If one of the stone is missing, they would have replaced with another stone and prayed with the same reverence. There were trees around the 'Idols'. They were praying the stones and life around as gods. Nature and ecosystem are real Gods for them, which were sustaining life and created a living space. Ultimately their belief is that "God is in everything", including non-living things like stones.

DROUGHT

A Geo Spirit meet on leadership was facilitated for 50 children from Sri Aurobindo International School, for two days. The children from 8 and 9th classes participated in it. There were girls and boys. It was in the year 2009, there was a drought prevailing due to scanty monsoon rains. The farmers in parts of Telangana State, India, were suffering from the impact of drought. The sown seed has not germinated much and the saplings were drying. The standing crops have wilted or dried in the fields.

Considering the severe drought situation, drought was chosen as the theme for the Geo Spirit meet. Before going to the field explained children about the prevailing drought and asked them to refer to media reports and books for understanding the drought. They were invited to prepareposters on drought in groups.

The field visit was planned at Chempak Hills and surrounding areas covering some of the severe drought affected villages. A few teachers have accompanied the students. The children were asked to go in groups and visit the villages to interact with the farmers on the situation of drought and its impact.

By discussion with the villagers, children learned some interesting things. The birds could sense drought ahead and the weaver birds have woven their nests hanging low in the open wells. During drought situation, the open wells don't get filled full. Therefore, the bird nests are made hanging low. These birds build their nests in open wells, on the hanging branches for security to the eggs and chicks from predators.

The standing crops were found dry. The green leaves turned brown. The sorghum plants became poisonous with an accumulation of cyanide. Therefore, the farmers don't allow their animals to eat them.

There were full water level marks in the water tanks and open wells, which indicate the water has not recharged till now. Indirectly these markings indicate the drought situation. The farmers' hardships during the drought have been understood by the children.

In the end, the children were asked to make presentations on their observations. Their expressions were so authentic and from their heart. It appeared as though for the first time that they understood the challenges of making a living with vagaries of nature and unsustainable agricultural practices. The books could have never taught, what environment taught them. At the end, they were sensitized to drought and environment. The children were asked to declare their choice of profession in the future. Most of their parents wanted them to become engineers or doctors, but they have declared all types of professions such as – Doctor, Engineer, Scientist, Writer, Teacher, Journalist, Lawyer, Politician, etc. But none of them wanted to be a farmer although they understand the importance of farming and have respect for farmers.

EARTH LEADERS NETWORK

Earth leaders are the people involved in environmental, ecological, social and developmental challenges of the earth. Most of these leaders 'if not all' represent non-formal and unorganized - institutes, agencies, organizations or committed individuals. To organize the earth leaders 'Earth Leaders Network (ELN)' is proposed, some of the aspects of the earth leaders are given below.

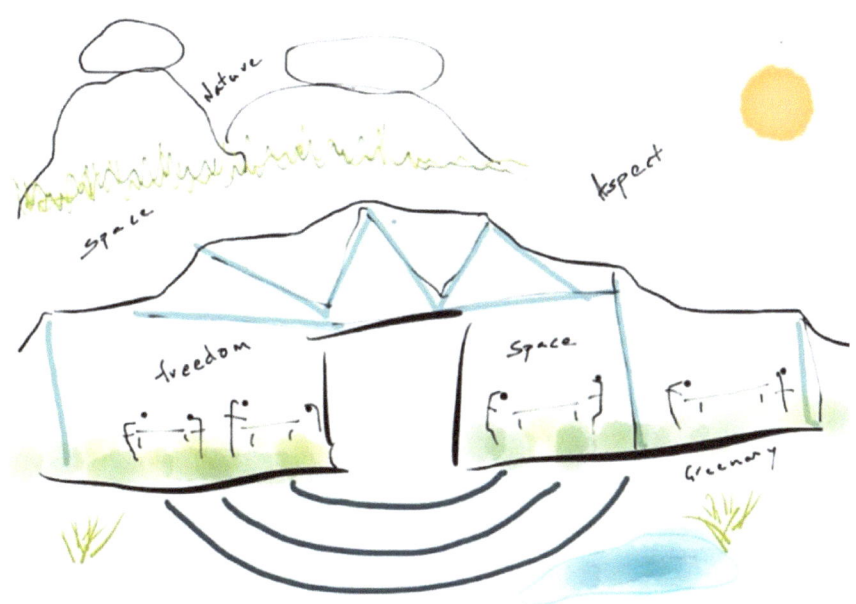

Serving the earth must be regarded as the highest form of service. Common goals are bigger than the personal goals. Earth leaders are committed to serving the earth in their own way. They could be surviving with meager resources. However, with the kind of selfless efforts they own and value, each and every part of the earth. They work as torch bearers to safeguard earth's very existence.

This is a network to bring together all those committed and working for the earth with the purest intent, under one umbrella for the following objects:

☐ For the earth leadership.

☐ To encourage young people to be the earth leaders

☐ To enhance their commitment.

☐ To facilitate earth leaders' communes in complimenting individual efforts to a collective force for a greater impact that is measurable and sustainable.

☐ To reduce the vulnerability of the earth leaders

☐ To enhance the knowledge and skills of the earth leaders, and encourage sharing.

☐ To enhance earth leader's capitals vis-à-vis Human, Social, Physical, Financial, Environmental and Natural.

☐ To promote professionalism in serving the earth through volunteerism, fellowships, scholarships, internships and professional platforms.

☐ To create a directory of the earth leaders transcending geographies.

☐ To create 'Earth Leaders Institute' for capacity building through awareness, sensitization, knowledge, skills, mobilisation, organisation, networking, and institutions development.

☐ To disseminate and exchange – values and best practices.

☐ To build the capacities of the earth leaders with seamless access to technology that will help them to organize their efforts and conserve resources.

GEO INITIATIVES

Geoecology Energy Organisation also known as GEO is an organization founded by the author. Mr. Lloyd Helferty, Engineering Technologist, Canada, observed that initiatives by GEO as follows:

"Personally, I like the approach of the Geoecology Energy Organisation (GEO) in Hyderabad, India. They have chosen to promote the creation of Sacred Spaces in every village they go to. These Sacred Spaces are specifically identified ancient forests and other natural landscapes that are intended to be preserved, not only for the mental health of the people, but also (literally) to protect and preserve Soil diversity and health -- and, thus create a legacy that ensures both food and bodily health. The 'body' of the earth itself -- is held sacred. They call these spaces, 'Geo Spirit Centres', where people care for and come to respect Mother Earth. In the literal sense that the word 'earth' is also a synonym for the soil -- which means that literally, they are places to protect; places where people can come to respect and care for Mother Earth, which literally could mean respect and care for the Mother Soil. And if you think about this -- really think about it -- it is true that the soil is really our Mother ~ for, without healthy soils, NO LIFE (on land) would Exist. And once we have created what we might call these Mother Soil sanctuaries -- the Spirit Centre's where soil (microbial) biodiversity is encouraged and left to flourish -- we may then get an opportunity to use "tools" like biochar compost that has been 'inoculated' by the Mother Soils, to help restore our badly degraded lands.In this case, heat sterilized biochar could be considered the "carrier" of soil biodiversity ~ allowing the abundant microbes from the Mother soil to [literally] be 'carried' ~ transferred ~ as intact as is possible, from the point of origin [the Sacred Spaces], and be placed on the degraded lands, to act as the 'seed' that can then re-populate these essential microbial communities back into the degraded landscapes."

MUSINGS

Musings cutting across all aspects of life, are for contemplation for the earth leaders.

HUMAN

Human beings evolved over years and were not the original creation on this earth. Even Gods might not have been in the form of human being.

All the knowledge acquired by people in one's own lifetime is finite. People are the most vulnerable species compared to many other species living on this earth. If ants had been more intelligent and powerful than the people, our gods might have been in the form of 'ants'.

Human beings belong to the species Homo sapiens in Latin means "wise man" is the binomial nomenclature.

We, humans, restrict ourselves and live a life with less freedom. People are selective and political too. "Human being," in which 'being' is continuous. Being in 'Human Being' is 'Sensitivity'. Only one species on earth is 'being'. To assert the expected nature of humans, human being term is used. Only humans spend time for being something. All other life on earth is 'living' a natural way of life. For example, there is nothing like 'dog being' for dogs. Because the dog is like a dog always in space and time. The dog has more freedom than human beings. A dog enjoys every space in the home than we do. A dog can sleep under the bed or in the bathroom or everywhere, whereas you can't. Whereas humans are 'being' based on their own understanding, conventions, convenience and norms of living. In each individual's life, being human varies in space and time. Say, a dog lover is more concerned about dogs, than cats or humans.

SENSITIVITY

Being sensitive is the greatest ability of human beings. A sensitive person is more useful to the society. Being sensitive consistently would lead to vision, knowledge and action.

A child immediately after birth responds to change in environment by crying. One is witness to the drastic changes happening to the beautiful environment. Many people are so mean and do not respond to the environmental changes. Whereas a child can react, but learned people are insensitive to environmental changes.

Often people are sensitive to only a few things of one's interest or ignore or not at all sensitive to other concerns of significance to Geo Spirit. The level of sensitivity also varies in space and time. It is based on the interest, duration of exposure and experience. Sensitivity might lead to awareness, knowledge, acquiring skills, understanding, and action. Being sensitive is a great boon for flourishing and realizing one's goal and to lead in any facet of life. Siddhartha Gautama being sensitive sacrificed everything to understand why life is full of suffering and finally realized and became the Gautama Buddha.

One glorious day as Siddhartha went out of the palace to the pleasure park to see the world outside, he came in direct contact with the stark realities of life. Within the narrow confines of the palace, he saw only the rosy side of life, but the dark side, the common lot of mankind, was purposely veiled from him. What was previously conceived only mentally, he now saw in vivid reality for the first time. On his way to the park, his observant eyes met the strange sights of a decrepit old man, a diseased person, a corpse and a dignified hermit. The first three sights convincingly proved to him, the inexorable nature of life, and the universal ailment of humanity. The fourth signified the means to overcome the ills of life and to attain calm and peace. These four unexpected sights served to increase the urge in him to loathe and renounce the world. We all might have seen many such sights, but how many of us have followed his path for the world. One might be sensitive, but a genuinely sensitive person leads to action and causes results.

Buddha helps us to understand the highest value of sensitivity. Similarly, one can be sensitive to different issues such as gender, climate change, global warming, social backwardness, poverty, etc. and work for mitigating the impacts.

IDENTITY

Don't ever have only one identity. Enjoy every facet of life by being present. Identity makes one imprisoned and sucks life. Identity is like ear markings on an animal.

A butterfly transforms and loses its identity and appears beautiful. The surprise of transformation from creeping caterpillar to a flying butterfly makes it more beautiful. Jack of all, lives a complete life compared to the master of one.

There is no freedom of thought and deed in beingcompelled to be someone. In one life many challenges are accomplished, it is like taking rebirth many times in this very life. Being curious and having many lives in one life is the real freedom in one'slife.

To achieve things, big or small, a person need not think that he will do everything to be in the limelight. If not the Loudspeaker, one could be the Mike - a source for the Loudspeaker.

Looking good and really being good is very rare. People deceive others by looking too good sometimes. The body language, spoken words, acts, etc., may not always be truthful. Looking good without any reason is rare to see among people.

CHANGE

If someone is stuck, sometimes continues to enjoy a given situation and seldom ready for a change. People get used to a particular situation - lifestyle and work, and they do not want to change. An insect living in the sewerage loves it. It never explores the other world and possibilities. Similarly, some people like what they are. However, a leader consistently explores the possibilities and works for positive changes.

LIFE

Life is simple don't make it complicated. Think today is your last day and do what all is possible. Life expands through knowing, knowing and knowing. There are always challenges at every stage ofone's life, overcoming them is what life is all about. Life without a goal has no meaning.

When one is alive, bad things are highlighted, after death good things are remembered. In one's life, more time is spent on bad things than on good things – discussed and shared. Good people spend less time on bad things. Too much is bad, some aregood and too little is poor.

When one thinks I am wasting time in my life, it is time to change. Life and time are limited, one may not fully understand the components of a car, but drive and enjoy.

Before and after nothing, there is something in between that is life. One who can value every moment in life can do only good. Giving is the complete meaning of life. Time is a relative term: 'less time' or 'more time' or 'no time' is based on the priorities of oneself.

There are moments in life. The meaning of life is an understanding of one's own past, being in the present and planning for future. The Past is the history, the future is planning and the present is to act – just do it.The real meaning of life is to be conscious and be happy.

We are living in a world of truth, false, belief and imagination. We all enjoy everything - right or wrong. To be a philosopher, one need to filter the truth from trash. This is a lifetime task.

MODEL

For encouraging students to be the future leaders, students are exposed to several case studies including the personalities who have accomplished in life. a) A person from a rural area, studied in a government school, with great hardships didPh.D., and now working in a multinational company. He is now earning well, and having a comfortable life b) A person from a village background, who was poor, once upon a time. Went abroad for a better income and now CEO of several companies. c) A person from a middle-class family, who struggled and studied well from reputed colleges. Although had the potential to get a 'decent' job, to the surprise of everyone, one day decided to work for the rural communities and on environmental issues. d) A person from village never went to school, but practicing sustainable agriculture. A source of inspiration for many farmers; never made wealth but living happily. e) A person struggled hard and achieved a government job as Agriculture Officer, automatic promotion and salary hike is ensured. Holidays, leaves and health insurance are taken care. Responsibility is least for the failure of the crops, farmers falling into the debt trap for increased inputs, and even farmers committing suicide for losing everything.

Each person is great in their own way, a child should not follow others' lives, but should choose on their own. The choice is the fundamental source of freedom.

KNOWLEDGE

One has born on this earth empty, understood something and made a life. One has no right to hold knowledge through patents and copyrights.

Knowledge is eternal and infinite; it is like the river that flows. It should not be held by the interest of few. For every creation, innovation and design, one should acknowledge all those who have contributed to that thought and knowledge; living or non-living things in the universe.

Open Knowledge is a set of principles and methodologies related to creation and sharing of knowledge in an open manner. Share as much as knowledge, it is never going to deplete, it will always be enhanced.

Open Knowledge is a source of freedom and integrity. The whole world is expanding at a rapid phase in all aspects of knowledge and technologies, the requirements of better and efficient technologies are also growing. The ecology is unable to sustain the needs of the people. People are not intelligent enough to copy and replicate nature in spite of so much science and technological progress. The natural creations are the ultimate sources of sustenance for life on earth. The very few technological innovations created by humans are also not accessible to all because of the following two main reasons. a) Self-interest or selfishness for social, economic, etc., considerations b) Investment made for the innovation.

What if while looking at the apple falling from the tree, Sir Isaac Newton picked up the apple and ate it and he did not delve on the gravity and discover laws of Nature. The whole world would have been different. Probably someday someone would have discovered the same in a different situation. Many discoveries and inventions do exist on earth but, everyone is not clever to have been able to patent. And geographically mainly the North American and European countries had these patenting systems in place since the 19th century. The holding of the knowledge by few is a hurdle for those who could have been the source of similar innovations. The knowledge in the hands of a sharing person is better than in the hands of a selfish person. It is bad to hold knowledge and not be able to share in the public domain when it is pertinent to the whole world.

If the knowledge is keptas apatent by someone, there are three options a) Use of knowledge by the source person b) Share the knowledge with others c) Sleep over the knowledge thinking that someday, I will use it. The majority of the times the last is in practice, for which there is no action of any kind against the person who is doing that. Anything not shared is like a "Drama without audience" – Thinking that one day I will do it myself is a great loss to the world. Preachings are meaningful only if lead to action.

The internet is one of the greatest communication tools of this century. In the history of human beings, the creation of the digital world is unique and it would continue. The access to knowledge is not limited, one could easily refer, copy, generate and understand. The copyrights and patents are not stringently honored. To protect patents and copyrights, nobody can fight battles in so many courts and countries. It is better to declare an innovation as Open Knowledge especially if it is meant for common good.

Patents and copyrights are ruling human decisions and development. The regime of patents leads to the creation of wealth for some. No knowledge has been created without following the principles of science existing even before humans were born on this earth. Appreciation of once contribution to the pool of discoveries and innovations is required.

Many people are the monkeys of desire trapped in a cage, not having the freedom to give up what one has. Traditionally monkey catchers use a technique, where monkeys are cleverly caught by placing a banana in a cage or a hole. Only the hand of a monkey fits  through a small hole in the cage, after holding the banana placed inside, as bait, the monkey cannot take out its hand. The monkey is trapped in its own desire to possess the banana and it is held there losing all its freedom. The monkey catcher catches it before the monkey runs away.

Symbolically, where banana is the knowledge accessed by the people not willing to share and trapped in their own desire losing all the freedom.

Open Knowledge is significant because it is declaring open beyond the source, which gives freedom for all. Open source technology, Creative Commons, Open source hardware and open design also gives one freedom. Liberation from source gives one greater freedom.

Open Knowledgeis all about solidarity and concern for this earth. Everyone loves the freedom of thought and act, Open Knowledge is the source. Let us declare things relevant to millions of people and the environment as Open Knowledge.

Some points for thought: People download more information and upload very less and useful information into the public domain. Collected data, knowledge, and information,is stored on their hard disks, emails, drop box, etc., There is no value after their death. There are so many global challenges faced by humanity, environment and ecology it is not right to hold knowledge relevant to make this earth a better place. There are many issues relevant to more than million people living on earth, at least, all the knowledge related to these millions of people should be declared as open knowledge. The governments, organizations, agencies should compensate the respective sources if needed and declare as Open Knowledge.

SHARING

Let us expand beyond boundaries by sharing. Sharing gives freedom to oneself and to the whole world. It gives immense satisfaction when we share fresh. One cannot compete with someone who wants to share. Sharing when one has less has more meaning than when one has plenty. Sharing is meaningful if it is "not for you and not about you". Teaching is enhancing sensitivity and interest in the pupil through sharing knowledge.

Human beings are not the Gods nor the creators of the universe. Everything works on this earth based on the laws of nature.

The discovery, innovation, design, process, etc., all are eligible for patenting. In the patenting system recognition for one's work and economic benefits are some of the primaryadvantagesof the person or organization. Patenting retards the progress and development. The laws of patenting and the following rights originated in the west, where the development of latest science and technology happened very rapidly. The basic science foundations were developed in the past. Nothing is in isolation, everything is interconnected from microcosm to macrocosm. Creations, innovations, discoveries in time and space are not discrete they are an integral part of the whole. No laws are different from what is existing in the universe. No other creature on this earth patents except humans. Patenting is an exclusion method for personal gains. Denying the right over laws of nature.

In the long run,patents, would kill the spirit of development. Let us share the knowledge and our creativity as commons for a better world and bliss. The more one shares, the more one receives.

Sharing types
- Authentic Sharing - It is complete and intentional sharing
- Intentional sharing - Selfless sharing and it is a push factor
- Selfish sharing - Only some aspects are shared and never one would know the whole.
- Bait sharing - Sharing attracts others to the source of complete knowledge.
- Proxy sharing - sharing the original idea with amendments and declaring as their own.
- Comfortable sharing - Sharing comfortably with only a particular section of people and who are non-competitive.

WORK

Work should be enjoyable, productive and lead to more work. Some people say they have done the work but with no results irritates many. Some people seem to be very hectic and doing lots of work, but the results are not meaningful for the efforts invested. All the species on earth work with their maximum efficiencies. Some people think they deserve the honorarium for attending the job. The majority of species do not exploit their own species as much as the humans do. Work is worship is to be preached to people who are lazy or in search of secure jobs. The day one has done productive work, one would share happily with someone they love.

We have to do something in life, so just do what you love. But real love manifests in doing not for you and not about you. If one has to live on earth, the resources and environment are helping us to live. And one has to work for all.

DUTY

If earning money is one's ultimate goal in life, then one's job is very hard. The job is described as the principal activity in one's life that one does to earn money. Money is a myth between real and unreal values. Money should be one's demand and command, one should not become the slave of money.  Loving money does not mean that money loves you.

Earth will not be abundant if one earns. The richer the people, poorer the earth.

Love your job not a day of work. Many people want to have a job. One of the principal reasons is security and money.

The social force that binds one to the courses of action demanded by that force is duty. The duty of a person is invaluable, it is altogether having a different value system, beyond monetary concerns. Duties are declared under the job, but most often they are not mandatory and only act as guidelines. Sometimes duties extend beyond time and space. Job and rights are always together. Sometimes, the rights of a job clash with duties. Many people in Government services are doing simple jobs. The responsibility of Government employee most often ends up with the right to a job and the privileges of that job. Sometimes the costliest services delivered are the government services, because of inefficiency. For the failures, it is rare to find a Government employee taking responsibility on their own and resigning from a job.

INCOME

The development interventions should always look at the short and long term impacts. A micro-finance institute should look beyond the payment of loans and mere economic development of its stakeholders. The source of income is most often from the immediate environment directly or indirectly. The access to resources by one stakeholder might impact accessto the same by another. The resources might get sometimes damaged beyond sustainability in the process of maximizing income. Always the development should be non-exploitative and sustainable. One should relate and analyze the revenues and sources of income while formulating the programs. This principle being looked at a micro-scale is also relevant to any other action and activities at macro-level too. Income term does not exist in nature, it is a creation of human beings, leading to non-sustainable development.

HAPPINESS

Some people are very happy, some are not so happy, some are sad but pretend to be happy and some are not at all happy in a given situation. On the whole, it is the degree of happiness. Why it happens? Say, a poor happy villager got a chance to spend one week in a luxury hotel, as he has come to attend a seminar on poverty and development. His stay and hospitality werewholly sponsored by the funding agencies. The farmer learned that the total bills accrued amount is equal to all that he earns in one year as income. He goes back to the village. Now he has some real experience to compare with his past and present lifestyle. How happy he is now??! How happy he would be to lead rest of his life?! Due to globalization and communication, many such scales are emerging into the minds of people. Do we think the whole world is much happier now than in the past?!

BACKLOGS

A doctor cannot give prescription now for a past ailment. One cannot sleep days together now to cover up the past sleepless nights. We need to shape rod only when it is hot. We live now and only now. One can always take steps for the future and not for the past. Say, if we don't have memory, history, records; in what way our past affects the present.

What is the punishment value for a person committing theft - a young person; the 80-year-old person; and committedthe theft at an early age and was caught only at an age of 80 years; or the fact was known after the death of that person. In the history of those individuals, the remark is the same, that they are thieves. But the young person sent to prison immediately after being caught matters the most.

PROGENY

The beauty of life is the progeny. There is no continuity or existence without progeny. The ultimate goal is to secure the life of this offspring, for which we put all our energy and efforts. All life on this earth exists for the same purpose. Unfortunately, some  species become extinct, as the environment over a period acts against its own nurtured adaptive capability to survive through evolution. Sometimes some species of birds, fishes and insects lay more eggs during an uncertain or unfavorable condition in the hope that at least few of their progeny survives. It was found that the poor people in countries with high child mortality rate tend to have more children. One of the reasons is they could see at least few surviving by the time they are adults.

The present environmental changes caused by one single species "Human Beings" is threatening the existence of many species on earth and already is the cause of extinction of many species. The "progeny" purpose of all life is at stake.

YOU

You are you. Where ever you are, you are you. The value of you is same everywhere. The value of you assessed by others might vary. Also, what I am is defined by where I am in time and place.

Wherever a personis should remain truthful and committed. If you are not there, it is their loss and others gain. The monetary value is one of the values for the work done in one's life, but not everything. Poverty, a measure in economics, need not lessen pride of the people. They might have greater values among themselves. The total some of the values around an activity is the real value. All the values around a subject are also important.

Say, God, in the form of a statue located at a place, has some value. If the same statue is replicated as original and placed everywhere, what is its value? If it is transported to another location what is its value? If copies of original statues placed everywhere what is the value? But for the God pervading everywhere has the same value.

One's kids are loved more than one's own parents. "Selfish Gene" dominates sometimes. It is rare that efforts, time and investment are made to save the life of elderly people. Although there are possibilities to advance death by selling all the properties. Most often to keep wealth for the young, old people are not taken care.

WELFARE

If governments take complete social responsibility, there is no need for any other organizations. Governments are permanent management agencies with their sources of funds from the collection of taxes, printing of currency, getting credit, charging for services, owning or partnerships in corporations, leasing resources and selling assets. There is a difference between government, organization, foundation, agency, corporation, Public Sector, Private Sector, and contractor. There is a social aspect to everything that the Government does. The government is permanent and it is an accountable system compared to any other thing. The government staff gets paid securely independent of efficiency and accountability. They are the last persons to leave the country in case of distress migration. If the government is a real social welfare state, there is no need of civil society organizations and private companies working in the areas of education, health, etc. Hope one day it happens!

The government is not loved by all equally. The public representatives, government employees, and contractors have a close bond in accomplishing the tasks. Teachers want government jobs but never admit their children to the same school. It is rare to find permanent government employees managing canteens or hotels.

GOVERNANCE

The government systems globally are becoming more and more inefficient, that is one more reason for increased expenditure budgets every year. Creating government jobs is not important unless we reduce inefficiencies. There is nothing to be happy for increased annual budgets by the governments, it means the same amount would be taxed or inflated through printing currency. Everyone would be taxed equitably through inflation including the poor. In personal life, it's hard for a person to have recurring payment commitments and struggle to live for paying. Then how come we are happy every year with increased taxes and per capita debt.

SPACE

Human beings in large numbers growing exponentially, require ample space for their own survival and thriving. The eight-inch-deep soil (earth), the atmosphere and the sea or ocean are the three important spaces for human beings. The surface area of the earth is increasing with physical constructions of multistory apartments. The domestic animals are caged in multi-layers for more yield of meat, milk, eggs per unit of area. Cutting down forest areas for agriculture; cultivating - multi-crops, multitier crops, intensiveshort duration crops; increasing gross cultivated land; intensive application of chemical fertilizers; use of chemical pesticides, etc., are the manifestations of the greed, demand, aspiration for more space and self-actualization.

REFERENCE

I saw a beautiful bird on the branch of a beautiful tree. Today, that tree was cut down and also the bird is not visible. The reference in time and space has disappeared. The kids of today have no such reference to the past. They can't imagine the beauty that once existed. They have a new and different reference How can we bring back that bird on the branch of a tree into the imagination of children? Conservation, protection, and promotion are best possible only through the records from the past. A 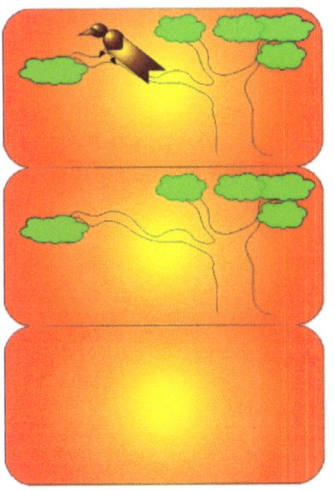 green paddy field for someone is beautiful but less beautiful for the one who has seen the conversion of a beautiful forest with wild animals into a paddy field.

The environment has changed a lot, the climate change and global warming is bringing lots of changes on earth. Manmade or natural changes are very much visible, measurable in one's own lifetime. To reconstruct the scenario and bring back things lost in time is nearly impossible. But to prepare for the future seems to be easier as an adaptation strategy. The problem with human beings is that majority of occasions we live in the past and expect future to be similar to our past, i.e., because we get habituated to a particular environment and expect the same situation to continue. We tend to like a given environment as we grow in it. The challenge is to change and adapt. Both change and adaptation happen in the process or through circumstances. At any given time, the sum of existing majority of species is the only most adaptive species.

COSMOS

The matter, as small as an atom, also has energy and rhythm in it. From micro to cosmos everything is a living thing. Earth is one of the smallest matter in the cosmos. Cosmos is a living thing. Within which there is the conversion of matter to energy and energy to matter. In between the two extremes of matter and energy is life. There is a harmony in the universe. People invest so much in exploring life on other planets and in the universe. One would be happy to find even a single living cell there. There is the cosmos with life in every unit of space on the earth. But we ignore and be the cause of extinction of many species on the earth.

ENVIRONMENT

The term environment is often used to the surroundings from the point of reference. Evolution of species was based on the changes that happened in the environment over a period of thousands of years.

The human beings are mainly responsible for altering the natural environment. People have recreated or altered environmentsto suit one's own needs through the use of technologies. These environments were artificially created by human beings. The home, workplace, etc., are all of the significant concern. The materials employed in the construction of residential houses were mostly natural in the past. At present most of the building materials are artificial and synthetic. Living spaces have an impact on the peace, health, socialization, happiness and spirit of the individuals living in such habitats. A home should also aspire one towards spirituality and also invoke one's spirit for the purpose of living.

The living environment for wild animals is not same as for man, it is a natural world required for biological needs and safety. Whereas human environmentsare a complex world that comprisesnatural, physical, social, cultural, political and economic processes and relationships. All the above environments cause an impact, of some degree in a person's life.

The Environment and Ecology terms are often used, there is a hierarchy of the usage of the words, based on the meaning, implications and impact. The term Geoecology (Earth and Ecology) stands at the top, which encompasses everything and holistic. Sometimes by having precisemeanings, we ignore the broader implications and one tends to focus only on the immediate concerns. Earth is the only planet, it is precious let us understand it more comprehensively as Geoecology, rather than limiting ourselves in understanding it through the use of shallow terms.

SUSTAINABILITY

The people over years have learned how to make a sustainable living from the available resources. Wisdom should be acquired by each individual, which should be evident in our being. That wisdom had greater meaning for sustainable life on earth.

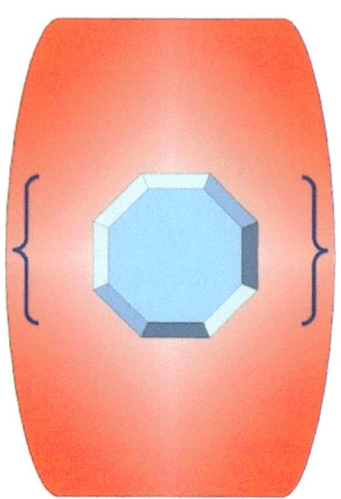

For example, the way of life of Bushmen of Kalahari or Eskimos of the circumpolar region in the North. If the "clever" people from urban areas were sent to those places, all the resources would exhaust within no time.

In the past all the places on earth were sustainable. At present, almost two earths are required to meet the carrying capacity of the earth. There is a lot to learn from each place how the practices worked earlier. The history still exists in every place, just open up and learn to create a sustainable present and future.

If sustainability is adopted by every living thing one earth as humans do, nothing would have been sustainable. Because thedefinition of sustainability owned and put into practice by people is "too much sustainability", those places become inhabitable within no time.

People are selfish, most often the priority of all acts are of concern to themselves. Sustainability is the term created by humans for their own sustainability. In this sustainability, only some species and resources do sustain. Human beings together constitute one big single living thing; the sole purpose is the sustainability of this living thing alone.

Most often the definition of sustainability is explained in terms of self-interest. The human-centricsustainability defined here is as perceived by the most "interested" people. The sustainability defined with someone's interest may not satisfy the interest of everyone. Sometimes interest makes a resource unsustainable. Too much interest is selfishness. The over-exploitation of resources, leading to the unsustainability of that resource.

If all the animals in a Jungle one day were taught about sustainability, as do human beings think. One alpha male tiger would herd all the animals it can eat, into one corner as a shepherd does put the sheep in a pen at the end of the day. Denying the right to other tigers as it owns them now. The super-sustainability of this tiger is achieved for generations and also for its progeny. Like some people amassing wealth for generations. The sustainable interest of one tiger is the non-sustainable issue for other tigers and other carnivorous animals. Similarly, if all the animals have thought about their sustainability, what would have been the sustainability of earth? The definition of sustainability adopted should be non-human centric, considering every biotic and abiotic resource on earth.

PEDAGOGY

For all life, the necessary things for making a livelihood are exposure, experience, skill, knowledge, understanding, and action. As part of the current education system, Human beings spend about one-third to one-fourth of their lifetime to get educated. Parents don't know in which areas their child is most interested. Children are too small to understand their interest, so they are forced to learn everything till 10th standard. But every child knows their interest in time and space. Their interest might vary with time as they grow. But the teachers and parents believe that the children are too young and they don't know what they want to be in life. And force them to choose areas, which they believe would guarantee secured livelihood. There is no system to encourage a child, have the freedom to set their own goal and strive to achieve, as they grow.

Education is useful for learning, awareness and knowledge. Experiential knowledge gained by children through education is very rare. In the modern schoolingsystem, the experience or practical's imparted to students is petite. Current education system would not help a child to live for a day in nature on their own. Ongoing education systems are making people more and more dependent. As far as survival skills are considered, the confidence levels of young generations are falling.

Pedagogy is the discipline that deals with the theory and practice of education; it thus concerns the study and practice of how best to teach. Its aims range from the general (full development of the human being via liberal education) to the narrower specifics of vocational education (the imparting and acquisition of specific skills). There is a need to evolve from traditional pedagogy.

Learning is never ending. Education is part of learning. There is an end to education but there is no end to learning. Only human beings get educated. Everything on this earth can learn even animals.

To evaluate a person's standard, the marks and grades are given in school. Standard of a person deteriorates with time and only in few areas they would be strong, which contribute to their livelihood or of interest. A person never gets same marks or grade, if they write an exam again and again. Many times they fail too. This education system tests and qualifies a person in time and space and never guarantees the 'standard' for a lifetime.

While teaching, a teacher always starts from lesson no. 1, in few subjects one need to follow a sequence. For some lessons and non-detail subjects, a teacher could begin the lesson as per the interest of the students. In that case, the focus and attention of children would be high. Their learning would be faster.

The questions appearing in exams are based on probability and cycles. Many questions arise as per the guess. A certain percentage of students pass the exam because the system cannot fail too many students. Otherwise the teachers and institutions are responsible for their failure. Over the years, the percentage of marks and grades are improving, but the standard of pupils falling down.

In real life, if someone has a problem or challenge, they apply their own learning, consult a colleague, refer literature, call a friend, etc. But in the exams, one need to write the solution on their own, without any other external support. A student should be given skills of all the means to find the best solution or answer to a question or problem to face in the real life situations. Rather facing the problem and struggling on their own. The evaluation of a person's ability to do everything on their own is not real education. The writing skills constitute a major method of evaluating the

students. Writing is most painful, people seldom write in their life. If writing itself is so unpleasant, why students are assessed by their writing skills.

Life skills are to be imparted on priority as part of education. Such as sowing seed, making clean water, catching fish, creating fire, cooking, sleeping under the open sky, etc. Sometimes a child from a village is more alert and active as compared to children born and brought up in the cities. The people educated through existing methods are highly vulnerable.

About 7 years back, I had been the course coordinator of Environmental Management module, for MBA students. I used to teach them outside the classroom – lecture on rocks, talk while walking in an industrial area, etc. I said the environment is an Open Subject - so for their exams, I have given them all the open options for writing the exam. i.e., refer a book, use the internet and call a friend outside. The students were happy. I gave them this chance of writing the exam on one condition, that only if they are also willing to give similar options to their students in the future if they ever teach.

Art, Science and Technology all are important. Say, an engineer designs a car with good engine and structure, but an artist finalizes the design of body with good shape and colour. A car designed only by engineers may not be appealing to the common public by looks. The engine and other inner parts which constitute 80% of the cost of a car are rarely seen and appreciated by people. But the outer body which represents 20% of the expense of a car is more appealing to the people and even to the owner. Very rarely we see people taking photos with the engine of a car. One might find more jobs and highly paid, by not studying arts. But all the subjects are important, as we have seen in the above case. Therefore, arts should be one of the subjects to study for the engineers too. To lead a complete life, one should know many things before one dies. Dying knowledgeable is better than dying as an ignorant person. Everything in this earth and universe is interesting and worth knowing. A generalist leads a complete life as compared to a specialist.

Ignorance is sometimes bliss. Because they never feel guilty, like a forest dweller hunting and eating a deer as done traditionally. But, for a person who understands that it is an endangered deer, he should never do that. Guilt, righteousness, and wisdom increase with knowledge and understanding of an individual.

FARMERS

By occupation farmer is the one who is connected with earth more than anyone else. Why a farmer is not honored, he is becoming more and more vulnerable? Over a period, this sector turned from sustainable agriculture to exploitative agriculture. The new practices are degrading the very resources which sustained farming. The soil degradation, water pollution, groundwater depletion, pesticide residues in the produce, greenhouse gasses release, etc., are some of the impacts. The scientific community and the policy makers introducing GMOs, chemical-based agriculture, etc., are also responsible for this pathetic situation.

If the budget component allocated to the farmers and agriculture sector increases every year means, we have not achieved much. If the annual budget allocation to the farm sector decreases, it means we are actually working and developing this sector. It is like the number of pills taken by a patient continues or increases, it does not mean that the patient is becoming healthy.

In the history, the farmers paid the taxes and contributed to the economy of the nations. Earliest civilizations and cultures in parts of the world flourished. The richest kings, kingdoms, monuments existed because of farmers' contributions. Today our policies, technologies, and other factors made the farmer no less than a beggar for everything - seeds, fertilizers, support prices, loans, insurance, power, rains (cloud seeding), water for irrigation, etc. There is a need for serious thought and strategy for the sustainability of farming and farmers' livelihood.

We love farmers and their well-being because they provide food, fodder, fiber, fuel and much more. Why we are not happy when the prices of their produce go up? There were jokes and anger when the price of onions increased. No one was bothered when the farmers had been at a loss many times, and even paying to dump the produce

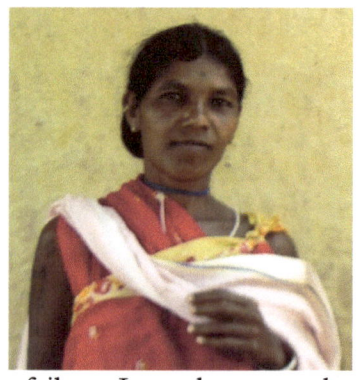

as garbage. I once dumped flowers as trash, cultivated on our Farm as the price was so low. In general, farmer rarely gets profits that he deserves for the efforts. Farmers feel sorry when the whole system conspires to bring down the prices when they rarely get a good price. On the whole, it is common sense to understand that the prices go high for various reasons such as a particular crop production was not high due to crop failure. In such a case, the farmer would get compensated through increase in price and so the dependent people.

First of all, every farmer deserves the right price for the produce. Paying the right price means we are not exploiting a farmer and also giving due respect to the farmer and the agriculture sector. A farmer lives happily with honor and dignity only when they could sell the produce at a right price with some profit, after deducting expenses on the inputs, labor, processing, etc.

The petrol and gold price also comes down, but not the water price. In the packaged water business, no one ever sayshow the price of a water bottle reduced. Even during the rainy season, the price of water is the same. There was never an offer like: one bottle free for every bottle purchase; 20% extra water for the same price; or free gifts on purchase of a water bottle. When water is an important input for agriculture, why the produce of the farmer should be undervalued. The state ensures the minimum wages for people working in all sectors, how come the state has never protected the minimum wages of farmers, by ensuring the minimum support to the farmers. Where are the labour inspectors in agriculturesector.

In the history, farmers were givers, i.e., taxpayers and contributed to the GDP of the nation. But they are now at the receiving end. Over the last 50 years, the pride of the farmers was belittled by the systems. Everyone around the farmer is getting benefited through exploitation but not the real farmer. The government officials, university professors, research scientists, and civil society representatives are happy with their profession. There are multinational companies benefited by selling seeds, pesticides, fertilizers, technologies, processing goods and selling the produce. The brokers and other middlemen are also becoming rich. The debt-ridden farmers are becoming poorer and few are also committing suicides. The dependent secondary stakeholders are not supporting the farmers. Whenever there is a sudden increase in prices, in the interest of destitute people, it is the discretion of the government to subsidize the goods.

In the past there was pride to say "I am a farmer," because farmers rarely depended on the government systems. Farmer was independent before India got independence, but after independence farmer has become dependent. Our system failed in promoting Gram Swaraj, otherwise the fate of farmers would not have been so bad. Farmers before independence were paying the tax to the then rulers. None of the rulers nor kingdoms ever had any debt in the past. At present, every nation is in debt, in billions of dollars. The debt is also on just born babies and those yet to be born. And we never know when this debt would be cleared. The civilizations, culture, and traditions flourished with the development, progress of agriculture, and surplus food production. The great monuments stand testimony to the prosperous agriculture-based economy in the past.

In the past, the development systems based on the primary sector such as agriculture was more sustainable. All the communities existed as a social network and promoted farming. The farmers had pride. Since last two decades, the farmers' contribution to the economic development of the nation is least considered, although majority of the population is still dependent on the agriculture sector. This is because of undervaluing the price of produce and labor. With the green revolution, the farmer's dependency on the non-sustainable input systems increased. The increased production is at the cost of degraded environment and ecological systems. The ecological footprint of the farmer is growing. The contribution of the greenhouse gasses emissions from the agriculture sector is also increasing. The vulnerability of agriculture sector is growing from newer dimensions such as climate change, pollution, environmental degradation, GM crops, etc.

Today, the economy is becoming more and more virtual, which is based on printed money, petrodollars, shares, and inflation. The farmers are contributing to the real economy through production. Through right price to the farmer, we could restore the pride of their farmer and also address the food security of the nation. Then the farmers hand would be a 'giving hand' rather a 'receiving hand.' The farmers would give up all the subsidies, get paid worth their labour, would employ people, adopt technologies, pay for power and water, etc. They would be no more at the mercy of policies. The farmer would also pay taxes for the development of the resources and social security. Once again we would see debt-free nations.

We are not sensitive to farmers; they are taken for granted. The day will come when everyone realizes the basis of our own existence.

CHALLENGES AHEAD

Globally, the year 2016 is very crucial for steering the world towards the historic commitments made in 2015. It was an extraordinary opportunity to bring the countries and citizens of the world together to embark on a new path to improve the lives of people. The United Nations Climate Change Conference, COP 21 or CMP 11 was held in Paris, France, from 30 November to 12 December 2015. A historic agreement to combat climate change and unleash actions and investment towards a low carbon, resilient and sustainable future was agreed by 195 nations. The universal agreement's primary aim is to keep a global temperature rise this century well below 2 degrees Celsius and to drive efforts to limit the temperature increase even further to 1.5 degrees Celsius above pre-industrial levels.

At the United Nations Sustainable Development Summit on 25 September 2015, world leaders adopted the 2030 Agenda for Sustainable Development, which includes a set of 17 Sustainable Development Goals (SDGs) to end poverty, fight inequality and injustice, and tackle climate change by 2030. The 17 Sustainable Development Goals and 169 targets, demonstrate the scale and ambition of this new Global Agenda. They seek to build on the Millennium Development Goals and complete what these did not achieve. They try to realize the human rights of all and to achieve gender equality and the empowerment of all women and girls. They are integrated and indivisible and balance the three dimensions of sustainable development: the economic, social and environmental.

The above two decisions are most important in the present context of global uncertainties. Frequent droughts affecting the underdeveloped and developing countries; depleting freshwater water sources; land degradation; loss of biodiversity; increased inequities and poverty; and increased forced migrants, asylum seekers and refugees as a result of some of the above reasons. The 2 degrees' rise is a compromise by nations. At 2 degrees' rise, all the SDGs would become more vulnerable to address. 2015 was the hottest year, records of the hottest years are broken now. Submergence of islands and coastal areas; frequent droughts and storms leading to floods are some of the impacts to be experienced in the future too.

Global economies are highly volatile. The consumer based economy is a vicious cycle. Unemployment rate is very high in many countries even up to 40%. The Chinese economy, one of the largest global economies is in doldrums. Therefore, the dependent countries' economies are also in poor condition. The good sign is that there is less demand for oil. As a result, the oil price has come down drastically, after so many years. Less usage of fossil fuels reduces the global CO_2 emissions. Now it is the right time for countries to switch to alternative renewable energy sources. International Solar Energy Alliance formed at COP21 is a good initiative.

The governments taking sustainable development seriously should stop sacrificing the environment for economic benefits. The immediate targets under SDGs are massive, how do we source funds and establish systems to achieve them. The grassroots civil society organizations are disappearing. The international funding is discouraged. The corporate social responsibility funds are the primary sources of funds. In the areas of education and health, the sources of financing would be better. The polluting industries would rarely support the organizations working on environment and ecology. Finding civil society movements for the environment and ecological issues are rare. The movements and revolutions would be more common for livelihoods. The natural resources sustainability is of

utmost importance to all life on earth. Food security is an important concern, for which the farmers and the farming system should be sustainable. Farmers are highly vulnerable and soon there would be a shortage of 'farmers'. Each person should emerge as an earth leader for whom "ecosystem matters". We want institutes for earth leaders for harmony and good governance. The collective global leadership is rare to find. Several governments are taking the role of corporates and also civil society. The current leaders are too political and mean, not even able to represent their own people. Inflation is very high even in the 'rich' countries. Ways to strengthen the economies of countries through petrol, military might, consortiums and through interference in the policies of other countries are least healthy. The virtual currencies based economies would not last longer. The super-rich people would find themselves poorer than Bushman in Kalahari. New models and relationships between countries are emerging on the principles of "survival of the opportunist". In these systems, there are not many values and it is very dangerous. The whole world is already beyond the carrying capacity, becoming less 'human'. This earth is virtually divided into many 'earth's', with increasing borders and stringent laws preventing peoples' movement.

Each and every individual should strive for small ecological footprints. The way of living also matters, what we eat and how much we waste; per capita usage of water and energy; etc. To begin with, 2016 is a crucial watershed year in the history of Human Beings, for making right decisions and strive for the common good.

ACKNOWLEDGMENTS

I express my deep sense of gratitude to Prof. K. Purushotham Reddy, an Environmentalist, for inspiring me to work on the earth challenges and consistent motivation.

Grateful to Mr. Eddie Leong, an Earth Leader from Singapore who said that "…The book contains a lot of sensible thoughts and down-to-earth wisdom and much of your philosophy resonates with Zen…" I am very much thankful to Mr. Lloyd Helferty, Engineering Technologist, Principal, Biochar Consulting, Canada for understanding my work and constant encouragement. Am grateful to Mr. Chris Kajo, Coordinator, NYAWEST Kenya, who commented that "GEO SPIRIT is reckoning of true human responsibility. Leadership and doing right in its true meaning. Very captivating as instinct is key. I am Looking at this with interest, worth reading and practicing". I am also grateful to Mr. Frank van Steenbergen, Director at MetaMeta, Netherlands, for his encouragement to write books and also for publishing the books 'Understanding Stoves' and 'Biocharculture.' I am also thankful to Mr. Mamidi Bharath Bhushan for finer corrections of the text.

My endeavor with the communities in the two decades in parts of 18 states in India and abroad made me sensitive to the global challenges. I express my love and thanks to those millions of ordinary people whose suffering has sensitized me to think of the present and the future. The diverse environments and ecosystems embraced and immersed me as part of them, and I could feel and listen to their being. Thankful to all the Earth Leaders who participated in the Geo Spirit meets conducted in diverse natural environs. My thoughts on Geo Spirit for Earth Leadership strengthened during the Geo Spirit Meets.

I express my gratitude to my mentors, Earth Leaders, friends and well-wishers for their support in my endeavors. I would like to thank especially: Mr. Ashish Arora, Sahaj Foundation; Mr. Bhargava Annamraju, Environmentalist; Mr. Ch. Umamaheshwar Reddy, Environmentalist; Dr. Mrs. Chhalamayi Reddy, Educationist; Dr. G. Chandra Shekar Reddy, Indian Forest Service; Mr. Harish Amur, Educationist; Mr. K. Narsanna, ARANYA; Mr. K. Laxma Reddy, Council for Green Revolution (CGR); Ms. K. Leela Laxma Reddy, CGR; Mr. J. V. Sharma and Dr. K. Thulasi Rao, Indian Forest Service; Mr. Pramod Reddy B., Environmentalist; Mr. R. Dileep Reddy, Greens Alliance for Conservation of Eastern Ghats (GrACE); Mr. Srinivas M., SSES NGO; Mr. Sunil Bhide, Sacred Groves Conservation and Rooftop gardens; Ms. V. Deepthi Reddy, IDHYA; Dr. V. Surya Prakash, Open House; and Mr. Y. Madhava Reddy, Vandemataram Foundation.

Would like to thank my sons Avan and Magh, for all their love. I also thank my wife and parents for their constant support and accepting my freedom.

I acknowledge and express thanks to my organization 'Geoecology Energy Organisation [GEO]', Hyderabad, India, that has provided me space on Geo Spirit.

June 2016   Dr. N. Sai Bhaskar Reddy
Hyderabad, India   saibhaskarnakka@gmail.com